Wild Weather
Blizzards

by Julie Murray

Dash!
LEVELED READERS
3

3 Dash!
LEVELED READERS

Level 1 – Beginning
Short and simple sentences with familiar words or patterns for children who are beginning to understand how letters and sounds go together.

Level 2 – Emerging
Longer words and sentences with more complex language patterns for readers who are practicing common words and letter sounds.

Level 3 – Transitional
More developed language and vocabulary for readers who are becoming more independent.

abdopublishing.com

Published by Abdo Zoom, a division of ABDO, P.O. Box 398166, Minneapolis, Minnesota 55439.
Copyright © 2018 by Abdo Consulting Group, Inc. International copyrights reserved in all countries.
No part of this book may be reproduced in any form without written permission from the publisher.

Printed in the United States of America, North Mankato, Minnesota.
092017
012018

Photo Credits: iStock, Shutterstock
Production Contributors: Kenny Abdo, Jennie Forsberg, Grace Hansen, John Hansen
Design Contributors: Dorothy Toth, Christina Doffing

Publisher's Cataloging in Publication Data
Names: Murray, Julie, author.
Title: Blizzards / by Julie Murray.
Description: Minneapolis, Minnesota: Abdo Zoom, 2018. | Series: Wild weather |
    Includes online resource and index.
Identifiers: LCCN 2017939259 | ISBN 9781532120855 (lib.bdg.) | ISBN 9781532121975 (ebook) |
    ISBN 9781532122538 (Read-to-Me ebook)
Subjects: LCSH: Blizzards--Juvenile literature. | Weather--Juvenile literature. | Environment--Juvenile
    literature.
Classification: DDC 551.555--dc23
LC record available at https://lccn.loc.gov/2017939259

Table of Contents

Blizzards

Blizzards can be dangerous! They can make road conditions unsafe. Icy roads and blowing snow can make travel impossible. Blizzards can cause serious car accidents.

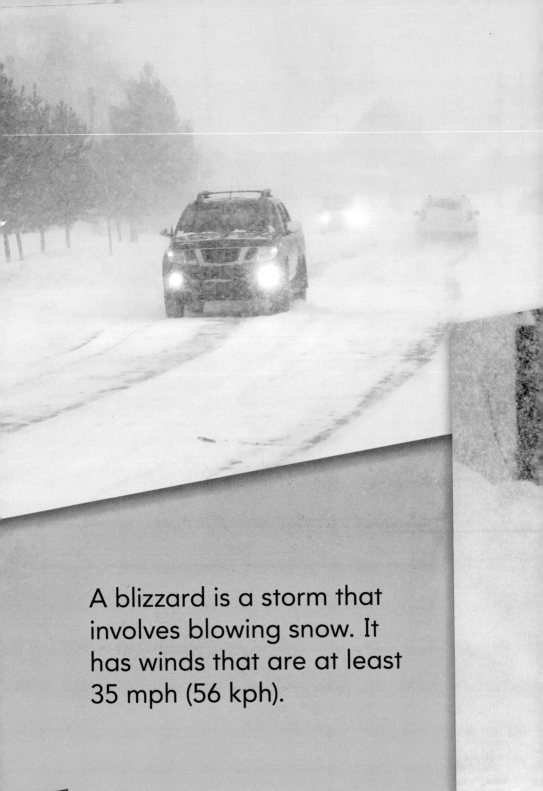

A blizzard is a storm that involves blowing snow. It has winds that are at least 35 mph (56 kph).

These winds blow for three hours or more. The blowing snow reduces visibility to ¼ mile (0.4 km) or less.

Not all blizzards occur when snow is falling. Strong winds can blow snow that is already on the ground.

This is called a ground blizzard. It creates conditions that can be very dangerous.

Blizzards occur when warm
and cold air masses **collide**.
The warm air rises above
the cold air.

This produces clouds, snow, and strong winds. The strong winds blow the snow around causing a blizzard.

Blizzard Dangers

Blizzards can create many problems. Large amounts of snow can cause roofs to **collapse**.

Blowing and drifting snow makes traveling on roads difficult. Strong winds can knock out power to thousands of people.

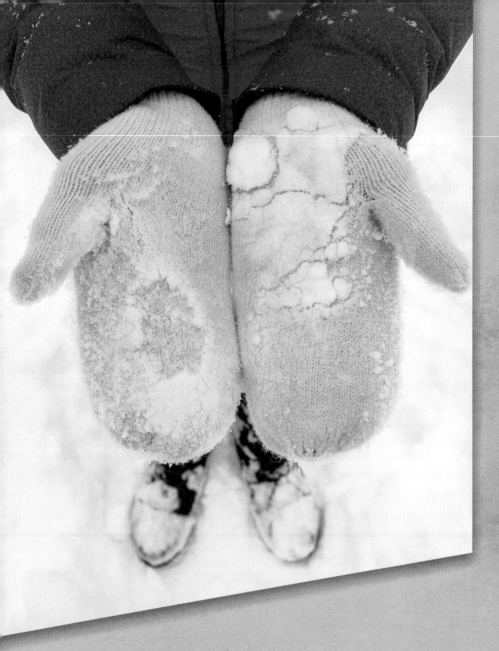

Frostbite is another danger
during a blizzard. It is the freezing
of your skin from extremely cold
temperatures.

Fingers, toes, and feet are the most common areas affected. Frostbite can happen within minutes.

Predict & Prepare

Montana -8 North Dakota 29 St. Paul 35 Detroit

-10 Wyoming 39 Des Moines 37 Indianapolis

7 h 11 Denver 20 Kansas

36 Santa Fe 25 Atl

34 enix New Mexico 33 35 Dallas 42 Montgome

Meteorologists can **predict** when and where a blizzard will occur.

They use radars, satellites, and **weather balloons** to track storms. They are able to warn people when a blizzard is coming their way.

Preparing for a blizzard is very important. If you are traveling in a car, make sure you have extra supplies.

A shovel, water, flashlight, and blankets are a must. These items could save your life!

What is the best way
to stay safe during a
blizzard? Stay home
and stay off the roads!

Many schools and businesses close during a blizzard. Enjoy a quiet day off at home!

- Tamarack, California, holds the record for the most snow in a calendar month. 390 inches (9.9 m) fell in January 1911.

- The snowiest city in the U.S. is Syracuse, NY. It averages 110 inches (2.8 m) per month December through March.

- The 1993 blizzard is called the "Storm of the Century." It affected half of the U.S. Snowdrifts were 30-40 feet (9-12 m) high!

Glossary

collapse – to fall down or cave in.

collide – to bump into one another with force.

meteorologist – a weather forecaster.

predict – say that a specified thing will happen in the future.

weather balloon – a balloon used to carry instruments into the sky to gather meteorological data in the atmosphere.

Index

Online Resources

Booklinks
NONFICTION NETWORK
FREE! ONLINE NONFICTION RESOURCES

To learn more about blizzards, please visit **abdobooklinks.com**. These links are routinely monitored and updated to provide the most current information available.